WHY SAY NO WHEN MY HORMONES SAY GO?

Emily Parke Chase

☧ CHRISTIAN PUBLICATIONS, INC.
CAMP HILL, PENNSYLVANIA

☖ CHRISTIAN PUBLICATIONS, INC.

3825 Hartzdale Drive, Camp Hill, PA 17011
www.christianpublications.com

Faithful, biblical publishing since 1883

Why Say No When My Hormones Say Go?
ISBN: 0-88965-196-5
© 2003 by Emily Chase
Printed in the United States of America
All rights reserved.

03   04   05   06   07   5   4   3   2

Unless otherwise indicated, all Scripture quotations
are taken from the Holy Bible, New Living Translation,
copyright 1996. Used by permission of
Tyndale House Publishers, Inc.
Wheaton, Illinois 60189.
All rights reserved.

*Note: Italicized words in Scripture quotations
are the emphasis of the author.*

Dedication

For all those young people, especially those who
are renewed virgins, who have the guts to
say no to sex outside marriage.

Contents

Five

Six

Author's Note

In the following chapters, some names and facts have been changed to protect the privacy of the individuals who have shared their stories. Names that appear in quotation marks, for example, "Joy," have been altered and should not be associated with individuals whom the reader may know personally.

Preface

"Sex is natural. Go for it! After all, you're in the prime of your life."

"No, you should wait for sex until you are married. It'll be more special."

"Yeah, you should wait, but we know you're going to do it anyway. Grab a condom. Take a pill. Protect yourself."

 Lots of people talk about sex, but what do you do if the messages contradict each other? Parents say one thing, school says another, TV and music say something else. Which message should you listen to?

If sex is natural, why can't you enjoy it before you marry? If you're supposed to wait, why do you have hormones racing around your body now? If sex is so good, why do you need protection? And why should you read this book if you've already had sex? Isn't it too late?

As you read the following chapters, the answers to these questions should become clear. No birth control pill, no condom, no shot can protect you from the kinds of pain described in this book.

Sex is good glue. When a man and a woman have sex, it bonds them together like superglue.

I work at a pregnancy center and I sometimes ask young people who come into my office about the first time they had sex. Every person, male or female, can remember that event. For some it may have been a negative experience where someone pressured them to have sex. For others it may have been a positive experience where they chose to become physically intimate. But each person can tell me an amazing number of details. They can recall colors, textures and scents. And they can always remember the day after. These memories can last a lifetime.

If someone rips a bandage off your arm, it hurts. When a sexual relationship breaks up, both people get hurt—no one walks away free of pain. After you've had sex, you carry memories from that relationship into the next.

What happens if you try to reuse that bandage that was ripped off your arm? It doesn't stick as well as the first time, does it? Sexual superglue also weakens with each new relationship. Each time you bond and break up, more memories accumulate. You bond; you break up. You bond with someone else; you break up.

Finally you meet the partner of your dreams, the person you want to marry. You want to enjoy sexual intimacy in your marriage, but suddenly you discover that the "glue" no longer works very well. All the memories of past sexual partners intrude on your intimacy with your spouse.

Think about it. Sex itself is not something bad or dirty. Sex creates an awesome intimacy. But if people ignore how sex works, the way God designed it, they will get hurt and will miss out on the true pleasure of sex in marriage.

This book is designed to help you enjoy sex to its fullest, within marriage. And, if you should happen not to marry, these pages will introduce you to a God who can fulfill every desire for true intimacy.

Acknowledgments

Thanks go to the many unseen participants in this venture: Gina Dalfonzo and Carmen McCain who edited early versions; Guy Condon, president of Care Net, whose suggestions resulted in major changes; authors Jim Watkins and Molly Kelly who encouraged a new writer; Esther Vannoy who did final edits; and the myriad of "I'm Worth Waiting For" college students who shared their stories.

Special thanks to "Randi," "Joy" and "Ann" whose personal stories have deeply enriched the pages of this book.

Ange, Ethan, Harold, Mildred, Myrle, Peggy, Robyn and Ruth, your faithful prayers have been answered.

Immeasurable appreciation goes to my husband, our children and my parents for their continual patience and encouragement.

Ultimately, thanks go to God Himself for allowing me to participate in His work.

The Story Begins:

Nothing but the facts

The names are changed, but this story, no matter how unbelievable, is true:

 "Hi! Call me Al. I can't tell you my real name because my dad's a big military expert over in the Middle East . . . lots of secrecy and stuff. If this story got out, he'd be in real trouble. He's in with the political scene, knows all the top people and speaks the languages better than most natives. Growing up in our house was like living in the U.N. I teethed on Hebrew and Arabic but some day it's all going to pay off. I'm sitting fine. Dad's going to retire, and I'm the natural person to step into his role. In the meantime, I just relax and watch the world go by."

"Don't pay attention to Al. I'm Tami. I grew up in the Middle East too, and I've known Al all my life. Al's the most eligible guy around. He's rich, smart, well-known and obnoxious. Sometimes my friends beg me to introduce them to Al, but frankly, he's a bit overrated. Well, I'm outta here. See ya."

"Thanks a lot . . . for nothing, Tami. See you around. Seriously, just between you and me (now that she's gone), I have to admit Tami's right about one thing—females flock to me. But the truth is, there's not a one of them that compares with Tami. Did you look at her just then? I mean, like, *really* look at her?

She has a body that just won't quit. No other girl within a hundred miles even comes close to looking as good as she does. Whoa, baby, what I'd give to be alone with her! There are nights when I just want to grab her and. . . . Sometimes I even forget to eat when she comes over to our place for dinner. What's a man to do?"

"Um, Al? Who are you talking to?"

"Oh, Jon! You startled me. Sorry, I didn't hear you come in. I was just telling my friend about Tami. I can't get that woman off my mind."

"Get real! Listen, you have everything you could want—money, women, a great future. You want tickets to the Super Bowl? Drop a hint and your dad will find some. You want a new sports car? It's yours. But Tami? No way. She's like a kid sister!"

"I know it seems crazy, but Jon, I've just *got* to find a way to get her alone!"

"So fake like you're sick. Ask your dad to have Tami stop by. You're alone in your room. You know what to do."

And that is how it happened. Al pretended to be sick. Jon brought Tami to the room and then slipped out the door. When Tami came near, Al pulled her close to his chest. His fingers groped at her waist.

"Wh-what are you doing?" Tami protested, trying to pull away. "No way, Al! Don't do this to me! Don't you care about how I feel? What about your dad?"

Al's only answer was to grab at Tami's blouse.

"Stop it! If you don't care about me, what about yourself? You could go to jail for this! How's this going to look when the press gets hold of it during a political campaign? Head-lines screaming, 'Candidate raped childhood friend!' Think! Don't be stupid!"

But Al didn't listen. Tami's loose top ripped as Al pushed her on to the bed.

The rape didn't take long.

When he was done, Al pushed Tami aside. "Get out of here," he snapped.

"No!" cried Tami, frantically trying to cover her body with the sheet. "You can't just send me out that door, go on with your life and pretend this didn't happen!"

But Al pulled her out of bed, opened the door and shoved her into the hall, calling out, "Jon! Get her out of here!"

The door closed with a thud; a lock slid into place with a dull click.

 Chew On It:

1. Jot down some words you would use to describe Al.

2. What words describe Tami? Was she to blame for what
   happened to her?

3. Al thought he was in love with Tami. Would you agree?
   What words would you use to describe his feelings for her
   at the start of the story?

4. What do the following sentences from the Bible tell you
   about God's feelings for you?

   And I am convinced that nothing can ever separate us
   from [God's] love. Death can't, and life can't. The an-
   gels can't, and the demons can't. Our fears for today, our

worries about tomorrow, and even the powers of hell
can't keep God's love away. Whether we are high above
the sky or in the deepest ocean, nothing in all creation
will ever be able to separate us from the love of God that
is revealed in Christ Jesus our Lord.

(Romans 8:38-39)

Other Thoughts

Do you know someone who was raped or hurt as the result
of a sexual relationship? Write a story about how that person
was affected by the incident? (Don't use any names—you
might want to share this book with other people.)

one

He Speaks

"Frankly, it was a pretty stupid thing to do. Here I was, set for life. I had a great career laid out ahead of me, and I blew it. I can't believe I lost control! I mean, I lost it all for less than an hour with a girl!

"But it's not as if it were all *my* fault. It wasn't like I really hurt Tami. I only did it once. As far as I'm concerned, it's history. I say we should just move on and forget it. But, no, Tami gets all worked up and races off to her brother. She says that I'm to blame. Then he tells my dad. Now her brother won't speak to me and neither will Dad. Women! They really can mess you up."

Is It Love or Lust?

Al never did express regret to Tami for what he did. For a long time it seemed like Al would get away with raping Tami. Even when his dad found out, nothing was done. No one talked about punishing Al. Everyone seemed to think, "Yes, it was an unfortunate event, but these things happen. After all, it was just the two of them. Just a private event." That's what Al thought too.

Some people would call Al a "stud" or say he was "macho" to describe his conquest of a woman. But other people, when they heard the whole story, might prefer words like "jerk" or "scum."

Al probably would have used the word "love" to define his original feelings for Tami. Again, others hearing the whole story might choose words like "infatuation" or "passion" or just plain "lust."

How can we know the difference between love and lust when our own passions are aroused? Just how do you tell if what you're feeling is the real thing or if it's just a passing fancy triggered by overactive hormones?

Look at some of the evidence from the story of Al and Tami.

1. Is it physical?

What was it about Tami that first attracted Al's attention? Her physical features. She had this great body.

You know, being physically attracted to someone of the opposite sex is not wrong. Way back at the start of time, a man named Adam was pretty excited about a woman called Eve the first time he saw her. (They were both standing there naked, after all!)

We all want a spouse who is enjoyable to look at. That's normal! Can you imagine greeting your spouse at the door but first turning away to overcome nausea at the sight of his or her face? That's crazy!

Looks, however, have a way of changing. Consider your parents' high school photos. Have you examined their wedding portraits recently? Do they look the same? Of course not. Time alters our appearance.

You look great now, but, if you are honest, you have to admit that there will always be someone younger or better-looking than you who will appear on the scene. If your relationship is rooted solely in physical attraction, your relationship will be history when some other, more attractive person shows up. Looks are a factor in what attracts us to potential mates, but they are an unstable foundation for a permanent relationship.

Lust is based on physical attraction alone, and this is our first clue that Al was not in love with Tami.

There are other clues that tell us about the difference between lust and love.

2. Is it selfish?

Who was Al aiming to please when Tami walked into the room?

First, how did Al get Tami up to his room? He lied to his
dad about being sick. He tricked his own father into being a
pawn in his game. Then Al fooled Tami. This is a great way
to start off a relationship, right? Ask some of your married
friends how many of them used deceit as a way to impress
their spouse on the first date. Love doesn't need tricks, but
lust uses every means possible to obtain what it wants.

Lust uses more than lies to get its own way. It is willing to
use force. Al counted on his greater physical strength to overcome Tami. All is fair in lust and war, right?

3. Is the brain in gear?

Once Tami realized what was happening, she tried to get
control of the situation by reasoning with Al. Did Al listen? Did
he say, "Yeah, Tami, you're right. This is a pretty stupid idea after all. Let's go get some coffee and forget this ever came up."

No! Here is one more piece of evidence to distinguish between love and lust. Lust tends to short-circuit the brain. It is
as if the brain hangs up a big sign which announces, "Out to
lunch." Common sense flies out the door. Long-term consequences are forgotten. I mean, face it, raping Tami was not
what you'd call a brilliant career move on Al's part.

4. Does it last?

After satisfying his desire for Tami, Al kicked her out the
door. Lust, once it has achieved its goal, moves on to something else. It is short-lived. My husband and I have been married over twenty years. He's stuck around: That's one way I
know he loves me.

So, to sum up, the focus of lust is "self." Al didn't care about Tami's feelings, only his own. Lust never travels with self-control. It is "self" being controlled by desire.

Not all guys are like Al. Not all girls are like Tami. Young women can be overwhelmed by the desires of lust just as easily as young men. My husband recalls when he was single and a young woman chased him across campus. The chase resulted in her grabbing at his jacket as he fled. Buttons popped off!

"Jenai" was a young girl who came into my office one day. It was not her first visit to our pregnancy counseling center. In fact, she was asking for her seventh pregnancy test. So far all her tests had been negative. Each time the counselor on duty encouraged her to consider abstinence. Now here she was back again. I decided to be more direct than usual.

"Jenai," I said, "am I right that being sexually intimate with your husband would be an important part of your marriage if you were to marry?"

"Oh, yes, having good sex is really important to me."

"If you were to marry, just how often each week do you think you and your husband would have intercourse?"

Jenai looked at me in surprise. She stammered, "Well, uh, I guess seven or eight times?"

"OK, let's say eight times. Now, how long does it take to have intercourse? Half an hour? Twenty minutes? An hour?"

Again Jenai looked startled. "I don't know. Maybe twenty or thirty minutes?"

"Fine. Let's see, eight times a week at thirty minutes a shot. Hmm. That adds up to about four hours per week. Jenai, how will you spend the rest of your married life when you aren't in bed having sex with your husband?"

For the first time Jenai seriously considered my point.

"We'd have to sleep . . . and eat."

We subtracted hours for sleeping and eating. I gave her a generous nine hours of sleep per night!

"Well, we'd probably have to go to work," Jenai suggested.

"Right. I'll even give you overtime. Let's take off another fifty hours for work."

There were still over forty hours of their week that weren't accounted for. At last, Jenai was able to see that a relationship has to have more than physical passion to survive.

5. What is the end result?

Ultimately, lust results in pain. It may be the object of the passion who gets hurt, as Tami did. But many times the person who loses control of his or her sexual appetite ends up feeling pain.

Mark was a great big handsome guy. Any football coach would have jumped at the chance to get him on the team. He was studying in an engineering program at college, and his future looked bright—just as Al's did before he raped Tami. Then Mark became sexually intimate with his girlfriend. His passion wouldn't wait until marriage.

When Mark came to talk with me, he already realized what he had done. He regretted his brief episode of foolishness. When his brain came back from its lunch break, he understood the impact of his rash action. But by then the girl was already pregnant.

She planned to abort the pregnancy. Mark wanted to stop her before they made a second mistake. He was ready to take responsibility and deal with the consequences of his act.

He vowed, "I'll give up college, get a job and marry this girl. Anything! Just tell me how I can keep her from stopping the pregnancy!"

But there was nothing he could do. Legally, he was helpless to protect the life of his child. Mark sat in the chair before me with tears streaming down his face.

That is just a taste of the pain that follows lust.

Set High Standards!

What about you? How can you be sure what you feel is love? How can you avoid being fooled by lust?

Begin by making a list of all the qualities you are looking for in a spouse. Before your hormones shift out of neutral and while your brain is in the driver's seat, think through what you are looking for in a life partner. This is a good idea to do whether you're in a relationship or not.

You might start your list by examining your friendships. What qualities are important to you when you pick out a friend?

For example, imagine you had a sensitive secret. Now suppose you shared that secret with your closest friend. That person swears not to tell a soul, but the next day when you arrive in class, everyone is whispering and pointing at you.

"Did you hear about . . .?" they ask each other. "Can you believe he did something so dumb?"

Obviously your secret is out. How do you feel about your friend? What is important in a relationship? TRUST.

Or suppose a classmate spreads a rumor about you cheating on the math exam. Believe it or not, this time you really studied and you got the top grade. Now this person is telling everyone that you cheated. What is important to you in a relationship? HONESTY.

What other qualities are necessary? Keep adding to your list. Be picky. Be specific. Set your standards high. If you are only looking for someone with a pulse and no moss growing on his teeth, you are not being picky enough. Keep in mind that the higher you set your standards, the more likely you are to find someone who is worth waiting for.

Perhaps you want someone with a good sense of humor. Do you like to read? Do you want someone that you can talk to on any subject? Are you interested in sports? Would you be happy with a couch potato? What kind of a parent do you want for your children?

Add to your inventory little things that are important to you. This may sound absurd, but I wanted a husband who could play the piano because I was too lazy to learn to play. I hoped my husband would be taller than I am. (I was the runt in my litter—my mother was three inches taller than I am and all the men in my family are over six feet tall.) I also wanted a husband who would be more intelligent than I am—it would make it easier for me to respect him.

These items may sound bizarre, but I put them on my wish list. The list was not cast in concrete, some of the items were negotiable; I was flexible. But my husband, Gene, does play the piano, he is taller than I am and he got perfect scores on his college entrance exams.

Is your faith important to you? Would it matter if you were dating a person who was not committed to going to church? What will happen if you marry that person? What happens when you want to go to church on Sunday morning, but your spouse wants to sleep in? Suppose your spouse wants to spend money on trips to the Caribbean or wants to buy a sports car. You, on the other hand, want to contribute the money to a missions project. Marital conflict will arise when issues like this come up.

When you marry a person with different beliefs, it is like starting a marriage with a big boulder between you and the one you love. You have to hike around the boulder every time you need to talk about something important. After a year or two, one person tires of walking and gives up the effort; he or she sits down and refuses to budge. You may shout over the rock at each other for a time or communication may cease completely.

If the person who isn't interested in God sits down on his or her side of the rock, the spouse with faith has to walk twice as far to communicate. The temptation will be to give up your faith and move away from the rock altogether.

That's why sharing the same faith was not one of the negotiable items on my list. Having a husband who could share my walk with Christ was essential to me. But I was even more specific than just wanting someone who shared my faith. I wanted someone who enjoyed Bible study, who was enthusiastic about evangelism and who was knowledgeable about Scripture. One of the things that I observed about Gene as we dated was that people would always come to him with deep spiritual questions. He would immediately find answers for them in his Bible.

After making your list, what do you do with it?

1. Pray about your list!

Ask God to remind you of qualities to be added. For example, maybe you forgot to mention that you want someone who is responsible. The Lord may bring new items to mind. He can also help you prioritize the list into negotiable vs. nonnegotiable qualities. Where are you willing to give and take? God delights in helping us on big decisions. He is even more anxious than you are to help you choose a life partner!

2. Keep that list handy!

Put the list in a place where you will bump into it regularly. Tuck it in your wallet, tie it to your car bumper or tape it to your forehead. Before planning a date, review it to see if the person you want to go out with measures up to your standards. After a date, look over the inventory again. Now that you know the person better, how does he or she fit your ideal?

3. Put God first!

Remember that no one person is going to be perfectly trustworthy, forever sensitive, always there for you. Only

God Himself can fill that role. While you wait for God to bring the partner of your dreams into your life, develop a relationship with Him. Learn to lean on Him and explore His character.

Before I got married, I was a satisfied single. I was content with the work God gave me to do. He took excellent care of me. In fact, I was so content being single that when my husband asked me to marry him, I said no! However, the Lord used my list as one way of confirming that Gene was in God's plan for me. My list, created long before Gene proposed, was very specific, and Gene met all of those criteria. (Do you get the impression that I love my husband? Good—I do, and I'm very thankful that God showed me that Gene was the right man for me.)

Your list is something that will help you to grasp the difference between love and lust. Al was not in love—he lusted after Tami.

Chew On It:

1. Make your own list of qualities you want in a spouse. Remember, be picky!

2. Interview two couples you respect. Ask each couple what
   qualities they think are most important in their relationship. Consider adding these qualities to your list if they
   are not already there.

3. Using numbers one to ten (one being lowest priority, ten
   being highest), set priorities on each item you have listed.
   For example, "trust" and "commitment" might each be a
   ten; "sense of humor" might be an eight; "enjoying hik-
   ing" might only be a five.

4. If you are currently dating someone special, compare that
   person with what you are looking for in a relationship.
   Does your date measure up? If not, ask yourself if you

want to continue investing in a relationship which is not meeting your long-range goals.

5. How does God measure up to what you most desire in a relationship? Is He trustworthy? Using the word index at the back of a Bible, can you find scriptures that mention the qualities on your list?

   Example: Commitment

   Be sure of this: I am with you always, even to the end of the age. (Matthew 28:20)

   I will be your God throughout your lifetime—until your hair is white with age. I made you, and I will care for you. I will carry you along and save you. (Isaiah 46:4)

   Those the Father has given me [Jesus] will come to me, and I will never reject them. (John 6:37)

Other Thoughts

Use the space here and on the following page to jot down a story about a person you know who faced problems when he or she had sex with their girlfriend or boyfriend. (I suggest that you not use any names—you might want to loan this book to a friend.)

REAL LiFE

Kyle Brady, NFL football player with the NY Jets

When Kyle Brady began high school, he was wrapped up in football. He didn't think much about God. He was even too busy for girls. A lot changed by the time he graduated from Penn State and became one of the top ten NFL draft choices in 1995.

"In my junior year of high school, I became sexually active with a girl mainly because everyone else was doing it. My friends told me I was missing out. I was curious."

That relationship did not last. By his senior year he had a new girlfriend. "We said we loved each other, we were very serious, but the relationship was very physical."

Kyle left for college and ended up with a Christian roommate. While his roommate read the Bible, Kyle went out partying. He thought, "The Bible is an ancient book. It doesn't have any relevance for young people today."

Both Kyle and his roommate played on the Penn State championship team. Gradually Kyle's attention focused on his roommate's faith. After asking many questions, Kyle put his faith in Christ.

"Some people change overnight, but I was stubborn. My relationship with this girl was out of control. I wasn't faithful to her, and later I found out she hadn't been faithful to me. There was no

23

trust. At the same time I was reading the Bible and learning that God commands us to be pure."

Finally Kyle ended the relationship. "We were both upset, but when we broke it off I felt relieved. Now I know that real love is not just physical. There is so much more to it. It involves sacrifice."

Since that time, Kyle has chosen to wait for sex until marriage. "The memories of what I did are like scars. Sex looks good, but it ends up burning you."

Today the fans scream wildly when Kyle's team carries the ball down the field, but, in Christ, Kyle says he has found "something to cheer about for real!"

two

She Speaks

"How do you describe a pain so sharp it cuts your heart in two?

"After Al pushed me out the door, I stumbled down the hall and out of his house. I was numb for hours. At home, I remember taking a shower for a long time, but nothing seemed to wash away the hurt. Finally I went to my brother, Sam. I couldn't talk right away, so he just put his arms around me and held me until I stopped crying.

"I couldn't tell him what Al had done, but Sam guessed what happened. He became furious. Sam told me not to worry. He would handle things. He told me it wasn't my fault. He also told me to move in with him for a while so that this kind of thing would never happen again. I was so exhausted from weeping it felt good to have someone else take charge.

"Later, other feelings started to replace the initial shock. I felt humiliated. How could Al just use me like that? Then I began to doubt myself. Had I led him on, making him think that I wanted to have sex?

"Before, I thought I could trust a friend I'd known all my life. Now I don't know if I can trust anyone.

"I was angry at Al, yes, but also at God. These days I'm not even sure about God. Is He really as strong and good as everyone says? I always served Him faithfully and now this happened. What did I do to deserve this? Is God just? Where was God when Al raped me?

"I feel like Al robbed me of everything that's important to me . . . my peace of mind, my virginity, my ability to trust people, my relationship with God. It is all a big mess now. I don't know if the pieces will ever come together again."

It Doesn't Have to Be Rape!

Rape is a violent act. Tami quickly discovered that the event involved far more than just physical violence. It touched every area of her life and left her feeling vulnerable. Now she is afraid of forming any relationship with a male.

You don't have to be raped to experience feelings similar to Tami's. Every day of the week scared young people come into the crisis center where I work. The girls are afraid they might be pregnant. The guys fear they may have contracted a sexual disease. But they all struggle with the emotional fallout of sexual intimacy. They feel used.

"Mary" came to me one day for a pregnancy test. She had been sexually active with her boyfriend. The weekend before her appointment, her boyfriend walked into the place where Mary worked, only he had another girl on his arm. He was hugging and kissing this other girl.

Can you imagine the feelings that went through Mary as she watched her boyfriend? Choppy seas would be smooth compared to the typhoon of emotions that raced through Mary's heart. She described his betrayal with great bitterness and anger.

"Sounds like trust is really important to you in a relationship," I responded after hearing her story.

"You better believe it," she nodded vehemently. "If I can't trust the guy I'm dating, then that's it. We're done. There's no relationship."

In Mary's case, there was no rape. She and her boyfriend had eagerly sought physical intimacy in their relationship. Yet when trust was broken, she was hurt and the feelings of being used were just as real as if she had been raped.

"Mary, may I ask you a question? Suppose two young men want to marry you. One guy has been sexually active. The other is still a virgin. Which one would you choose to marry?"

It only took a moment for Mary to make up her mind. "I'd choose the one who was sexually active. He's got experience."

Her answer didn't surprise me. I'd heard it before from other young people. "Let me ask the question from another angle. Same two men. One has chosen to wait for sex until marriage. The other has been in bed with a variety of women. Which one would you trust more to remain faithful to you after marriage?"

This time Mary took longer as she pondered the choice. I felt like a brain surgeon watching her thought process. It was as if brain synapses were connecting for the first time inside her head. At last a smile emerged on Mary's face.

"I see what you mean," she replied. "I understand what you're saying, and, even though I hate to admit it, I agree. It would be harder to trust the guy who has been with a couple of women."

It would be harder to trust him. Not impossible, mind you, but harder. Mary's boyfriend had been in bed with her, and then, when he tired of her, he moved on to another woman. When he had enough of the second woman, he would probably go looking for someone else.

"Even if he marries me, it is hard to be sure that, when he gets tired of me, he won't seek out another woman," Mary continued. "I'm not sure I could trust him to stick around."

Why Is Self-Control So Important?

A wedding ring is not like an electronic dog collar. It will not zap a husband every time he looks at another woman. Nor will it keep a wife within her boundaries.

Not all the good-looking men and women disappear off the face of the earth when that wedding ring goes on. Temptations continue after marriage. Women won't stop making passes at a man just because they know he is married. In fact, guys often find the temptations increase after marriage because women may consider a married man more mature or committed (in other words, attractive!) than the single men they know.

There is no magic button on the wedding certificate which you press and suddenly—poof!—you have self-control.

Sexual self-control is something you practice both before and after the wedding. Did your favorite basketball star get an NBA contract by shooting a few hoops and bouncing a ball down the court? No. He practiced for years to develop his control of the ball. When he finally signed the NBA contract, he already had the skills necessary to fulfill his contract. If you make a habit of sexual self-control when you are single, it will naturally continue after marriage. Self-control is evidence that you have what it takes to be faithful.

"You mean that we have to have self-control after marriage too?" You bet. Did that basketball player stop having to practice just because he got an NBA contract?

"I thought that after you got married the problems were over. After all, you can have sex with your spouse any time you want."

Yes, to some extent this is true. But has it occurred to you that once you marry, you will not be with your spouse every waking moment of the day? Sooner or later one of you will need to run to the store! You might even have to go to work. You don't need to practice trust when you are together all the time. The real question is, "What happens to trust when you are apart?"

When a guy marries, his heartbeat still speeds up when that bikini-clad beach babe saunters by. No matter how faithful he is to his wife, his hormones kick in. If he never learned how to control his desires before marriage, how can he develop skills in five minutes at the beach?

How do you know your husband is not messing around with the secretaries at work? Are you sure your wife is being faithful during her business trip? If you get shipped across the ocean on a military assignment, wouldn't you like to know that your wife or husband is waiting for you until you get home? Knowing your spouse had self-control before marriage makes it easier to believe that he or she can handle temptations when you are away.

Perhaps you have never thought about the practical realities of the last months of pregnancy. Having sex when the wife is in the ninth month is awkward and uncomfortable. And after the baby is born, four to six weeks must pass before the woman is allowed to have sexual intercourse again because her body needs time to heal. How will your relationship survive two months without sex?

One of you may get sick. My friend Ange married Bob. Last year, Bob had to go into the hospital for emergency surgery. It was a messy piece of work. His appendix was swollen, ready to burst. Some of the infection seeped out into his abdominal cavity. It took several weeks before the doctors could get the infection under control and release Bob from the hospital. Did Ange stay at the hospital the whole time under his watchful eye? No. She had to go home and look after their kids. Bob, hooked up to IV tubes in a hospital bed, had to trust that his wife would be faithful to him.

Do you have the sexual self-control needed for such an extended period of time? One way to know if you have that kind of control is to practice it before marriage.

Do I Meet My Own Expectations?

In the previous chapter, I suggested that you make a list of qualities you would value in a lifelong partner. I encouraged you to set high standards. Take that list out once more. Look over it and see if you meet those standards. Are you willing to be completely honest? Do you encourage and build up those around you? And this is important: Are you trustworthy?

Trust is a two-way street. You need to know that your marriage partner is going to be faithful to you. But he or she needs evidence that you also are reliable when it comes to resisting temptation.

If you have not had sex, you have already shown you can resist pressure. Way to go!

What If I've Already Had Sex?

What if you have already been sexually active? Maybe you chose to be sexually active. Maybe you were forced into it like Tami. Does this mean that you have already blown it? You may be asking, "How can anyone trust me when I already messed up my life by having had sex in the past?"

Should we put you on the bottom shelf with reduced merchandise, like dented cans at the grocery store? What hope is there for you?

You Can Change!

Let me ask a few questions. Have you ever told a lie? (If you say no, you are probably lying right now!) Does the fact that you have told a few whoppers in your life mean that no one can ever trust you again? Does it mean that you have to keep on lying for the rest of your life? Of course not. How do you get people to trust you again? You stop telling lies.

Did you ever steal something as a child? Maybe some money disappeared from your mom's purse. Or maybe a candy bar mysteriously vanished from your grandmother's candy drawer. Just because you stole something once upon a time, does it mean you must continue to steal? Do you need to sign up for career courses on becoming a cat burglar?

Perhaps you were caught and discovered the negative consequences of your act. You made a mistake and decided to change. You moved in a new direction.

Terry is another friend of mine. He is in charge of an inner-city mission for young teens. When Terry was still a teenager, he spent time in jail for theft. One day, after sharing his life story with young people at his center, he asked them, "Now that you know I was a convicted thief, would you trust me to come into your home? Would you trust me not to steal money from your wallet?"

"Of course we'd trust you," the kids replied without hesitation. "You're not like that any more."

And they are right. Terry has changed.

Many young people are doing exactly that with their sexual behavior. They have stopped having sex and are saving themselves for marriage. So can you. It is called "renewed virginity."

Many of the clients who go to pregnancy centers are young people who grew up in the church. They have been hurt and crushed by their past sexual behavior. They don't like the consequences of their actions. They feel as attractive as a well-chewed piece of gum. If you feel used, you are not alone.

1. Get things straight with God.

Starting over begins when you seek God's forgiveness and healing for the past. God specializes in making new creations out of used material.

Whatever your circumstances, God can bring healing for your past. Perhaps you are the one who initiated physical intimacy, and now you carry a burden of regret. It weighs you down and makes you feel unworthy. Perhaps you were the victim, and your burden is a heavy load of anger.

"Randi" recalls, "I don't think I ever believed that I was worth waiting for before, in my old lifestyle. Down deep inside of me in my subconscious I didn't believe that a man would ever stay with me if I didn't screw around with him."

Randi went on to explain that every time she gave in to her date, the relationship deteriorated. "I can't explain it better, but all I know is that every time I fooled around, something happened. I couldn't get back what we had before the intimacy took place."

"Miranda" always planned to wait for sex until she was married. After she went to bed with her boyfriend the first time, she told herself, "It's no big deal." But years later she confessed that it was a big deal and she still felt the hurt.

Talk honestly to the Lord. Let Him open up that massive backpack you have been carrying around and allow Him to remove each item inside. Ask Him to wash you, and then leave all that heavy load with Him.

2. Make a commitment to wait.

Decide that you will wait for sex from today until the day you marry.

Molly Kelly speaks to young people all over the country about chastity. She asks them, "If you have given all your money away, what do you have to do? Start saving it again. Or if someone stole all your money, what must you do? Why, you have to start saving again!" It is the same with renewed virginity. If you gave away your virginity or if someone stole it from you, then start saving it once more. And like money in the bank, it will become valuable again. It will start to gather interest too!

One of the benefits of starting over and waiting until marriage is that it gives your emotions time to heal and your memories time to fade.

Imagine, for example, that you just got married. On your wedding night, you enjoy the intimacy of sharing your bed with your spouse. All of a sudden, memories of the last person you were in bed with come to mind. Those memories are the last thing you want in bed with you on your wedding night. They cause you to compare this night with other nights, your spouse with other people. Wham! Intimacy is destroyed.

And even if your own past partners are the farthest thing from your mind, if you know that your spouse was sexually active a short time before with someone else, you wonder if you measure up to their previous partners. What if your wife said, "Being with you was almost as good as when I was in bed with Steve."

It is not a pleasant thing to be compared! Sexual intimacy, which God designed to bond two people together, is torn apart by jealousy, anxiety, anger and competition.

Waiting for at least a year between your commitment to renewed virginity and your marriage allows those memories to fade. It gives you time to demonstrate that you have gained control of your desires. And it gives time for the intimacy of sex to become new again.

"Joy" is a young woman who now goes into schools with me to speak with young people about waiting for sex until marriage. Before she came to work with me, Joy began a sexual relationship with her fiancé. They were sexually active for two years before their wedding. A baby arrived ten months before their big day.

"My wedding day was such a letdown," Joy recalled.

"Joy," I replied. "I was at the church. It was a beautiful wedding! How can you say it was a letdown?"

"You saw us smile and wave as we left the church under a shower of rice. But what you didn't see was how we stopped the car after we drove around behind the church. I hopped out of the car and ran into the church to pick up the baby. Then we went home to our apartment. We didn't have money for a honeymoon. You see, I was pregnant again. All our money had to go to pay for diapers, formula and baby expenses. We didn't even have money for a babysitter on our wedding night!

"When we got home, the first thing we had to do was put the baby down for a nap. Then we did our honeymoon thing. There was nothing special about sex the first time after the wedding. No bells. No whistles. It was like every other time we'd had sex in the past.

"We napped for a while. Then we opened a few wedding gifts. Later friends stopped by. We all went to get some take-out food and then came back to the apartment and watched a movie . . . on our wedding night!"

That night, Joy cried herself to sleep. As she put it, "That night was such a disappointment. I realized that I had my honeymoon two years before the wedding."

Contrast Joy's story with that of another of my college students. I'll call her "Kyrstin."

Like Joy, Kyrstin was sexually active before she married. She had sex while she was in high school. Kyrstin never got pregnant or contracted a disease, but she was hurt when her relationships broke up.

After finishing high school, Kyrstin decided to become a re-newed virgin. Three years later, she met a wonderful man who asked her to marry him. He had been sexually active too but, like Kyrstin, he had made a new decision to wait for sex until he married. It was not easy for these two young people to keep their self-control during the year they were engaged. Kyrstin knew where to touch her boyfriend to arouse him. She had to be cautious with her hands. He understood that his words had a powerful effect on Kyrstin. Together they sat down and wrote out a contract that spelled out how far they would go and how they would deal with certain situations. And after signing it, they stuck to it.

Later, after the wedding, I wrote to Kyrstin and asked her about her wedding day. Was the wait worth it?

Kyrstin sent back a glowing letter. She said her wedding night was fantastic. It was everything she ever hoped it would be. "I thought I had blown it when I was in high school. I thought sex would never be special again. I was so hurt. But after waiting so long, the memories were gone and the hurts healed.

"In the hotel on our wedding night I looked at my husband and knew I could trust him to be faithful to me. I knew he respected me too for waiting so long."

I wrote once more to ask for a copy of their dating contract to share with the students I see in schools. Kyrstin replied, "I can't send you the contract. One of the things that made our wedding night unique was when we took out the dating contract in one hand and a match in the other hand, and we burned them in our hotel room. We knew we didn't need that piece of paper any more."

That's renewed virginity. It's an option for anyone, male or female, who has been sexually active outside marriage. Don't get me wrong. This renewed virginity stuff is not easy. It takes a lot of guts to make this kind of commitment and keep it. We'll talk about how to keep the commitment of renewed virginity in a later chapter. But admit it; you have got to admire someone who makes a promise like that and keeps it. You respect that person. And you trust him or her.

Remember Tami from our story at the beginning of the book? She never heard about renewed virginity. She was so devastated by rape and broken trust that she never did marry. It is not too late for you. Now you know that you can start over.

Chew On It:

1. Think of people you trust. What makes you trust them? Do they trust you? Why?

2. Imagine your wedding night. How will you make it different from any other night?

3. What might happen (emotionally, physically or spiritually) to a person who refuses to accept God's forgiveness for something he or she did in the past?

4. What do the following sentences tell you about God's ability to make you new again?

> We have stopped evaluating others by what the world thinks about them. Once I mistakenly thought of Christ that way, as though he were merely a human being. How differently I think about him now! What this means is that those who become Christians become new persons. They are not the same anymore, for the old life is gone. A new life has begun! (2 Corinthians 5:16-17)

5. A young single mom told me, "I'd rather be lonely than ever lower my standards again."

   If you stayed single and never married, like Tami, would it be worth not having sex just to avoid further hurt?

Other Thoughts

Write a few sentences about a person you know who became sexually active before marriage and faced some unforeseen consequences.

REAL LIFE

Andy Landis, country Christian singer

At 9 a.m. on April 22, a knock on the door interrupted Andy's breakfast. Grubbed out in red sweats, her hair still messy, she debated whether to open the door. But looking through the peephole, she recognized a friend she'd dated a few months back. . . .

Andy didn't think about not opening the door—he wasn't a stranger, after all. But after letting him in for a cup of tea, she felt a wave of fear wash over her. Her instincts were right. Soon he pushed her to the couch and raped her.

"How could I have known he was going to do that?" Andy says now. "Afterward, I went to work, pretending nothing was wrong. Somehow I felt that the rape was my fault, so I didn't tell anyone what had happened."

Six years went by, and Andy kept her secret locked up inside. . . . A record company began negotiating a contract with her. . . .

A contract was signed, and the artists who were to join Andy . . . included Twila Paris and Ricky Skaggs. But Andy agreed to do the album only on the condition that she be allowed to record "No," a song she'd written about rape. Here's the chorus:

> No, no, I wanna get out
> She says, no, no,
> that ain't what love is about
> She says no, no, I gotta get out

But he couldn't hear her
His hand was over her mouth.

"The first verse is about date rape," Andy says. "It describes a couple whose kissing in the backseat of a car gets out of control. The second verse is about stranger rape. They're very different, because date rape can damage your ability to trust friends."

Self-image is another thing damaged by rape. Andy says, "If we start to let our self-respect be further chipped away, especially in the area of boys, dating and sex, it will affect us for the rest of our lives."

Andy says, "If you think you've found the right boy, then wait. If you don't think he's the man for your future, you shouldn't be dating him anyway. And believe me, I know how hard it is to be that strong. But you've gotta believe the Lord has a plan for you. Let Him—not some boy from algebra class—influence your life. . . .

"The Lord never asks us to do something that doesn't have a gift at the end," she says. "He's not asking us to wait so we can shrivel up and die! And if the gift at the end isn't a husband, you'll have some other reward for following God's plan for your life."

From "No Stranger to Fear," by Susan Maffett, *Brio* magazine, July 1995, published by Focus on the Family. Copyright © 1995 by Focus on the Family. All rights reserved. International copyright secured. Used by permission.

three

A Parent Speaks

"When Tami's brother told me what my son Al had done, it seemed like an avalanche crashed down on top of me. Memory after memory hit. The first ones stunned me; then the load got so heavy I felt like I couldn't breathe.

"You tell me any parent would feel overwhelmed under the circumstances? You are right. I was outraged that my son had raped a young woman, a girl he'd known all his life. I couldn't believe this had happened in my own home.

"But so much more was involved. Things I thought I had dealt with and put in the past suddenly hit me with full force.

"You see, a few years ago I hurt a woman in much the same way Al did. She wasn't someone I'd known for a long time, but she was another man's wife. In fact, she was the wife of one of my closest associates at work. When her husband was out of town for a couple of months, I forced her to have sex with me. That event triggered the worst nightmare in my life.

"Before her husband returned, the wife told me she was pregnant. As a well-known public figure, I had to keep this out of the news. Doing that was harder than any military crisis I ever faced.

"I tried to fool her husband into thinking the baby was his. When that didn't work, I had to plan a cover-up. As his commanding officer, I assigned him to direct a covert military campaign. No one asked questions when he died after leading his men in an attack. Shortly after that I married his wife and claimed the child as my own.

"That, I thought, was the end of it. No one knew . . . except God. Even though I thought the crisis was over, God knew my secret, and He kept bugging me. Night after night, the memory of what I had done gripped me. I'd wake up gasping.

"Then the baby got sick. After all we'd been through . . . well, at that point I knew God was not going to let me get away with what I'd done. I did everything I could, but the baby died. After that two things haunted my dreams instead of just one: the death of my friend and the death of my child.

"Now do you understand why I reeled at the news of Al raping Tami? All these memories resurfaced. How could I blame Al for forcing a woman into bed when I was guilty of the same thing? How could I accuse him when not only had I raped a woman, but I had been an accomplice to murder?"

What If Mom and Dad Find Out?

Al's dad found that something buried in his past came roaring back to life when he heard about Al raping Tami. How could his dad blame Al for what he himself had done? How could he punish Al without also condemning himself?

Al's dad had watched one child die. If Al went to prison, it would be like losing a second child. Worse yet, Al possibly knew about his father's past. Al was old enough to remember the events. If Al's case went to trial, everything his father had worked so hard to hide could be exposed.

So Al's dad did nothing. His anger boiled, but he sealed it in a vacuum deep inside his own heart.

Sexual passion is hard to control and so are its ripple effects. What Al did to Tami behind a locked door produced hatred in Al and pain for Tami, but it also set off a chain reaction that affected their families and friends. Al's dad was horrified to see the ripple effect of his own past sexual passion.

If you have sex with your date, how could it affect your parents?

Suppose your pregnancy test just came up positive. Or your girlfriend just called to say she's pregnant and that you are the father. How will you tell your mom? Imagine her reaction and the questions she'd ask:

"I didn't even know you were sexually active! How long has this been going on?"

"Who's going to take care of this baby?"

"Who's going to tell your father?"

"What about your plans for next year?"

"What will people say?"

All these questions are accompanied by tears or shouts or icy glares. How would your mom feel? Hurt? Disappointed? Betrayed? Embarrassed? What about your dad?

A junior at a local high school watched two students act out this scene as a class project. This young man was already a father himself. After his female classmate finished telling her "mom" she was pregnant, the young man looked at the rest of the class and said, "It was 10,000 times harder than that when I told my mom."

A young woman who was no longer a virgin told me, "My mother is in heaven. I don't know if she can see everything or not like God can, but to think that there is a possibility that she knows what I have done . . . if she were not dead already, it would kill her!"

And guys, if you think it is hard telling your own parents, try telling your girlfriend's dad that you got his daughter pregnant! (Should I mention that her dad is a Marine?)

If you wait for sex until marriage, you'll never need to face this scene.

You know, you don't even have to get a girl pregnant to experience the ripple effects of sex.

Your parents are away for the weekend. Your date comes over. You are watching a video in the living room. The lights are down low. Hands start moving. Clothes start flying and the windows begin to steam up.

Pretty soon you are doing it—having sex right there in the living room. Unexpectedly, your mom walks in! No one is pregnant, no one has a disease, but all of a sudden, waiting for sex sounds pretty good, doesn't it?

How Will It Affect Them?

Many parents are like Al's dad. They have buried memories of their own past relationships. Perhaps they were sexually active before their wedding night and they don't feel they have the right to tell you to wait for sex if they messed up when they dated.

The parents of "Sandy" came to visit her on campus. When she told them her band would be playing at a local restaurant, they went along to hear her sing.

Sitting at a table listening to the music, Sandy's dad saw one of his old college friends walk into the restaurant. Waving to the friend, he invited him to sit down and join them at the table. Sandy's stepmom cringed. It had only taken a moment for her to recognize her husband's friend. She had slept with this man over twenty years before! As she struggled to make small talk, her nervousness was obvious to all at the table.

When they got back to the hotel, her husband confronted her. "What made you so nervous tonight? You looked really stressed out."

The stepmom made a hurried excuse, but her husband brushed past her explanation. "Was this the guy you told me about, the one you had sex with when you were in college?"

Sandy's stepmom felt trapped. "No," she lied.

Still her husband was dissatisfied. Reluctantly, she revealed the truth. Even though the event had happened twenty years earlier, her husband's jealousy burned. Her attempts to cover up the incident only made things worse, destroying his ability to trust his wife.

Think about yourself twenty years from now and imagine yourself as a parent. What advice would you give your son about sex? Will he be willing to wait if you didn't? Al's dad was married but that didn't keep him out of trouble, and Al ended up following his footsteps.

How Do You Stay in Control?

When you are physically attracted to someone, is it possible to stay in control?

Both Al and his dad hit hormone overdrive. Loss of control began with physical attraction. Al knew Tami so well she was like a sister, but one day he looked at her body and his hormones kicked in. Dad saw his friend's wife. He knew the woman was married, but her beauty blinded him. Al's dad could have said, "No, this woman is off-limits."

Someone once defined discipline as "living within the boundaries of reality." Al and his dad both stepped outside that boundary. They both allowed themselves to be tempted and then let lust take over.

Temptation is weakest when it first steps into the room. If you play with it and don't recognize the boundary that is about to be crossed, temptation gets stronger. Your common sense starts to shut down, overpowered by hormones.

Al and his dad, instead of squelching desire immediately, entertained the temptation by bringing it closer. Al's dad invited his friend's wife over when her husband was away. Al asked his father to send Tami up to his room. When they were up close to these women, smelling their perfume, temptation tightened its grip.

Recognize desire for what it is and say no right away. A U.S. Health Department brochure says, "If you think it is hard to say 'no,' just wait until you say 'yes'!" Give in a little now, and things will be even more difficult later. Deal with temptation at the start while it is just a mind game, before you ever get out on the playing field.

Randi, now a renewed virgin, told me about a time when she wanted to buy a porno magazine. "I played with that temptation, literally driving all over two towns looking for a place where I could purchase it without anyone I knew seeing me. I was allowing myself to play with the idea, allowing temptation to get stronger and stronger until I found what I was looking for. And between you and me, I was already completely turned on in the car before I even got the magazine and looked at the pictures."

Then she added, "Now that I have had sex, boy, is it hard to say no. The hormones are nothing compared to what it actually feels like. Talk about hard? This is hard!"

There was something else Al and his dad did that caused problems. Al's dad was alone with his friend's wife. Al locked the door once he and Tami were alone in his room. Bad idea.

Having other people around and staying in public areas are two ways to stay in control. Picture yourself at a high school football game. Halftime arrives. Can you imagine the couple next to you running out on the field and having sex right there in front of all the fans? Unless your school is unusual, this scene is unlikely to occur. Why? Because it is easier to stay in control when people are around.

I've asked a lot of teens how they keep their hormones from getting too hot and heavy. Here's what they told me:

Cambric doesn't wait until she's in the backseat of the car to decide, "Do I want to wait?" Before she ever gets out her front door, she has made up her mind about waiting until marriage.

Rachel says she avoids problems by being picky about the guys she dates. She doesn't go out with the kind of guy that wouldn't respect her. "I set high standards."

Scott is up-front with his dates about his plan to wait until marriage. He tells them, "I want to wait for sex until I'm married. I'm not going to pressure you for sex. I'd appreciate it if you wouldn't pressure me." Girls line up to date Scott. In fact, one girl came up to me on campus and begged me to introduce her to him. She'd heard that he didn't compromise his values and she wanted to get to know him.

Chad sets clear boundaries. How far can you go before you are aroused? Chad sets up a barrier and then stops long before he gets to that point. For example, picture the sports car of your dreams. You're out on the highway zooming along at eighty miles per hour—OK, officer, make that sixty-five miles per hour—when you crest a hill. There at the bottom of the hill you see that a tree has fallen across the road. When will you hit the brakes? When you're at the top of the hill, as soon as you see the tree, or at the bottom, ten feet before you hit it? If you delay, you might not stop in time. You could get seriously hurt or even die tangling with that tree trunk.

I can't tell you how many young people walk through my doors, ask for a pregnancy test and say, "I never meant to go that far." They raced up to the line, tried to put on the brakes at the last minute and ended up crashing through their own boundary.

Gina puts it another way: It is hard to stay on your diet when the waitress brings a hot fudge sundae to the table and sets it in front of you with the nuts and cherry sliding down the pile of whipped cream. Say no before it ever gets to the table! With sex, say no before you get near the boundary line.

Enlist reinforcements. Al's dad was a military man. He knew the importance of having extra manpower to back up his troops. He should have taught Al to do the same before Al raped Tami. If you are going to wage war against hormones, tell someone you respect about your desire to wait for sex until marriage. Enlist a parent, a grandparent, a friend, a sister or brother. Ask them to quiz you every time you go out on a date. If you really respect the person who is holding you accountable and know they are going to check up on you, you'll avoid crossing your boundary on a date because you would face embarrassment telling them you messed up.

"Ann" wanted to wait for sex until she was married. She knew that I spoke in schools about abstinence so she asked me, as a close friend, to hold her accountable. After that, I made it a point to question her every few weeks about how she was handling the physical side of her relationships. When she became engaged, my husband and I shared her joy.

Two months before the wedding, Ann blew it. She had sex one time with her fiancé and deeply regretted it. A few weeks later she discovered she was pregnant.

Ann's parents were divorced, so telling her parents was twice as hard. Instead of just two parents she had four. She and her fiancé had to inform his parents as well.

Then Ann had to face me. Tears streamed down her cheeks as she told me she was pregnant. She was confident that I still loved her, but we were both crying before she was done. She was disappointed in herself but, after telling me that she was pregnant, she felt like she had also stabbed her best friend in the gut.

Back up your decision to wait with both words and actions. For example, take an objective look at yourself in the mirror before you go out on a date. What message do your clothes send? Does the muscle shirt or the short skirt say, "Let's party"? If you don't want to party, don't send invitations.

Doug plans activities for each date he goes on so that there isn't a lot of free time. He says, "When you're just sitting there, hands start to move!"

Before you go out, formulate a clear picture of where you will go and what you will do together. You are going out to the coffee house. What happens then? Will you stop by a friend's house? Will you go home to an empty house? Which one will put you at greater risk of giving in to desires?

Be creative when planning your time together. One young man in Idaho asked his girlfriend if she would like to have dinner with him on a romantic island. She thought it was a great idea but, since they lived in the middle of potato fields, she wondered where he would find this romantic island. "Don't worry," he replied. "I'll pick you up at 6:00 p.m."

That night he drove her to his home. Out in front of his house was a traffic island. Cars went this way. Buses passed that way. There on the island were chairs and a table, a candelabra and a white table cloth. His mother came out and served them there on their private isle!

Did that girl know that this fellow liked her? Will she ever forget that date? Don't just plan a date. Plan a memory!

One more suggestion: Figure out ahead of time how to say "no." Tami kept her head. She already knew that her virginity was important to her. When the pressure was on, she was prepared with a list of reasons to wait.

Once when I was speaking at a school, I asked Chris, a peer presenter who volunteers with my program, to try propositioning a female student. Chris turned a thousand shades of red, much to the amusement of the class, but he managed to get the idea across. The girl, by this time well aware of the intent of the role-playing, looked up into Chris' face and replied, "No, I want to wait."

What happened next was unrehearsed. Chris whipped out his watch, checked the time and looked her straight in the eye. "OK, how about in two hours?" The class collapsed in laughter.

When you want to say no, make your standard clear. Over and over I hear my clients say after a pregnancy test, "I'm going to wait next time!" But I don't always believe them. That's because I know that they don't define "waiting" as I do. They mean they will wait until the scare of pregnancy has faded. Or they will wait until they know the other person better. Or they will wait until they are engaged.

How many people do you know who have gotten engaged and then have broken off the engagement? When I was in college, I got engaged to a young man. We thought we would get married, but then I wasn't so sure. We broke off the engagement. Later we got engaged a second time. We broke up a second time. Then we made plans to marry and broke it off a third time! The next year I met another man, the one who became my husband.

I thought that I was going to marry that first guy. There were opportunities to have sex; I thought that we would be together forever. But I ended up marrying someone else. Boy, am I glad I waited!

When you say, "I want to wait," make it clear that you want to wait until you're married. Not just until a better-looking person comes down the pike. Not until you are in the mood.

Not until you are in love. Not until you are engaged. But until you are married.

I have a poster in my files. The words say, "What to wear when you are planning on safe sex." The picture shows a young couple on their wedding day. The bride is wearing her wedding gown. The groom is in his tuxedo.

One young woman who visited my office was a beautiful Christian girl. She and her family attended church regularly. Years before, she made a deep commitment to wait. She even had a chastity ring which she had planned to present to her husband as a gift on their wedding night. But one night she lost control. She had sex and got pregnant at the end of her freshman year of college.

I asked her what advice she would give to young people about staying in control of their sexual desires. "Tell them it can happen to them."

Sexual temptation is powerful. You will never be strong enough to fight it on your own. All the boundary limits, human reinforcements and public areas you stay in are not enough. The ultimate weapon is a strong relationship with God. Never assume that you are strong enough to handle things on your own.

Pray before you go out on a date. Pray while you are on the date. Pray with your date.

Only in Christ, by the power of His Spirit, will you succeed where even military leaders like Al's dad have failed.

Chew On It:

1. Set a $10 budget and plan an evening of fun. Where will you go? What will you do? Could you still have fun if the budget were reduced to $5?

2. Think of several people you respect. Determine which one could hold you accountable to your decision to wait for sex until marriage. Ask that person to help you with your commitment.

3. How can you show someone you really care about him or her without using any physical contact? Why do you think

God said it is good for a man not to touch a woman? (see 1
Corinthians 7:1).

4. Look at the following sentences and summarize what
   God has to say about self-control.

   Remember that in a race everyone runs, but only one
   person gets the prize. You also must run in such a way
   that you will win. All athletes practice strict self-control.
   They do it to win a prize that will fade away, but we do it
   for an eternal prize. So I run straight to the goal with
   purpose in every step. I am not like a boxer who misses
   his punches. I discipline my body like an athlete, train-
   ing it to do what it should. (1 Corinthians 9:24-27)

5. How would you respond to the following pressure lines?
    "Sex is natural. Everyone's doing it."
    "Don't worry. No one will know."
    "What's the matter? Are you scared?"
    "Don't you love me?"

Other Thoughts

Do you know a story about a parent who was hurt because his or her child became pregnant or contracted an STD? Jot it down here as a reminder of the ripple effect of sex outside of marriage.

REAL LIFE

Lakita Garth, former Miss Black California

Lakita Garth grew up near a California housing project which writers of *Money* magazine described as one of the most dangerous places in all the country to raise kids.

While Lakita's dad fought in Vietnam, her mom kept a gun of her own near at hand. Lakita says, "My mother slept with two men every night . . . Smith and Wesson."

One day some teens were shooting hoops across the street. Her mother called the guys aside. "You know what, boys? There are two things I'd kill a person for. The first is if you break into my house. The second is if you touch my daughter."

Lakita laughs when she describes the impact of her mother's threat. Not one guy dared to ask her out during high school! (No one broke into her house either.)

Lakita went on to become Miss Black California and was even a runner-up in the national competition. With her looks, she could attract any man she wanted, but today she is still single and still a virgin.

She is holding out for true intimacy, not just sex. "Intimacy is the ability to be completely yourself with another person, to share your hopes, your desires, your dreams, your biggest fears, your worst failures. And you're not afraid that this person will laugh at you or talk about you behind your back; they will always encourage you to do what is right.

"One of the biggest lies we've been told is that love is the same as sex. It is not! Love is the desire to benefit someone else at the expense of self. Lust is the desire to benefit self at someone else's expense."

When she meets teens who are sexually active, Lakita challenges them, "Who is really paying the brunt of the cost in this relationship? Who is benefitting? Who is actually having to sacrifice their future? Who is having to sacrifice their emotional and psychological, not just physical, health?"

Lakita travels across the country talking to teens in schools and on talk shows. She passes on the same message her mother taught her, but she doesn't use a gun to back it up.

Quoted portions from a talk given by Lakita Garth at the National Leadership Summit on Abstinence, August 2, 1997. Used by permission.

four

A Brother Speaks

"When Tami first appeared on my doorstep I could tell something bad had happened. I thought that somebody had died or there'd been an accident or something. When I figured out what Al had done, I was ready to kill him.

"Of course, I told Al's dad right away. His face turned gray and he said he'd handle everything, but day after day went by and nothing was done. Al kept walking around like nothing had happened. His father never punished him. Tami kept crying. I don't see how she gets up each day or how she can face Al without losing it.

"I mean, where's the justice? I could report what happened to the police, but who's going to believe me? It's Al's word against mine.

"I'd always admired Al's dad. Now I've lost all respect for him. He has pull with the police and in the courts. Does he step in and see that something is done? No, he does nothing, *nada*. That's not justice.

"If I were in charge, I'd see things done fairly. If people came to me with problems, I'd see they got justice. A lot of politicians talk about getting tough on crime. Well, I'd do more than just talk. I'd get out there on the streets and arrest them.

"In fact, that's what I did. When nothing was done about Tami's rape, I decided to settle the score myself. I waited a long time so nobody would be suspicious. Al and I used to hang around a lot when we were growing up, so no one was surprised when I invited a bunch of guys, including Al, to go away with me for a weekend. Late that night, I had someone knock off Al quietly. Well, it was supposed to be quiet, but all hell broke loose.

"Rumor was that I'd killed all the guys, not just Al. That wasn't true—the other guys weren't hurt—but I split right away. No way was I going to hang around there. I was out of the country in twenty-four hours!

"At first the revenge felt good. I thought I'd solved the whole problem. I thought that justice had been served. It didn't work out that way, though. Al was dead, but I was still mad. The bottom line was that nothing undid the rape. Tami wasn't any better off. In fact she was worse 'cause I wasn't around any more.

"Al's dad and I didn't speak for three years, even though he knew where I was. Friends told me he understood, that he was sad 'cause he missed not just Al but also me. Couldn't tell you for sure if this was true; he never said anything to me.

"At last a friend spoke to Al's father. He got me an official pardon, and I moved back to town. Big deal, right? I never saw him. We didn't speak for another two years. Five years in all. Why, I'd gotten married and had four kids in that time. (I named my daughter after Tami.)

"Eventually I got sick of all the pretense. Al's dad was as popular as ever, even though one of his sons was a rapist. Give me a break! I decided to run for office. After all, no one could ever prove that I'd had Al killed. I'd never been convicted of anything. I was popular and good-looking. Pretty soon I had a lot of people behind me.

"Only later did I realize that everyone I worked with was somehow connected with rape. My campaign director's granddaughter was molested by, get this, Al's father! Joe, the fellow I chose to be head of security, was my cousin: Years ago my aunt was raped and became pregnant; she gave birth to Joe.

"There was so much hurt and hate in our office. Nothing we did ever seemed to lessen the pain. People say only Al died. But in a way, all of us are dead."

Who Else Gets Hurt?

 Can you sense the anger seething within Sam? His sister's rape had ended up controlling his life. In fact, after Sam's political campaign failed, he went ballistic, rebelled against authority and even raped women himself.

How could a guy who was a decent brother, who just wanted justice, get so messed up? He wasn't the one who had sex in the first place. How come he got hurt?

A lot of innocent people can get hurt by the ripples of passion.

Gina called me one night in tears. Her sister was in an abusive relationship and had just discovered she was going to have a baby. Gina couldn't concentrate on her studies at college because she was worrying about her sister. She exhausted herself running home on weekends to help out.

Mary Beth's older sister had always dreamed of going to Europe for a summer. The plan was to bum around the continent with a backpack on her back, visit the sights and stay in cheap hostels. But Mary Beth's sister got pregnant instead. Now instead of studying at college together, Mary Beth is away at school while her sister is at home caring for a baby. They are missing out on a lot of fun times together.

Joy's sister became pregnant after she dated a guy for a short time. Joy felt hurt when her mother assumed that Joy would become sexually active just like her sister. Even though Joy had planned to wait for sex until she got married, her mother's low expectations of her had a negative influence: Within a year Joy also had a baby.

Pam's sister isn't pregnant, but she is sexually active with different partners. Pam worries that her sister might contract a disease. Her sister's lifestyle has affected their relationship. They used to talk about everything together, but now Pam's sister won't even speak to her.

Worry, exhaustion, lost trust, lack of communication: They are all part of the fallout parents and siblings feel as a result of the ripple effect caused by misplaced passion.

These are some of the effects people discuss openly, but what about real anger? Tami's brother, Sam, was angry because Al hurt Tami. Sam's anger smoldered below the surface. While most people do not have to deal with the anger that results from the rape of a loved one, lots of people do get angry when their brother or sister chooses to be sexually active.

Julie saw that kind of resentment fester in her best friend, "Chris." Julie says, "I remember when Chris' sister Laura announced that she was pregnant. Chris watched her parents, friends and all the members of the church rally around Laura. A baby shower and financial help made Laura the center of attention."

It was worse when the baby arrived. Chris resented it when Laura played with the baby and left all the housework to her. The baby's cries at night woke everyone in the house. Chris had to get up early to catch the school bus while Laura slept in with the baby. Their mom would say, "Chris, be quiet. Laura had a bad night." Chris' sister made no plans to seek a job to support herself and the baby. She seemed happy just to stay at home.

Can you blame Chris for being angry? She was suffering the consequences of her sister's sexual behavior.

What about the financial pressure a baby puts on the whole family? Will there be money for you to go to college or will it all go to support your brother's baby? What will your parents spend money on, diapers or a diploma?

Let's say no one gets pregnant as a result of premarital sex. Pregnancy isn't the only thing that can happen. The sexually active family member could contract a disease. Getting a disease can be not only a financial burden, but can be an emotional one as well. How would you feel if you had to tell your friends that your brother or sister had AIDS? Many families don't share that kind of news because they are embarrassed when people find out. Secrets like that can be a great burden on the entire family. What if people find out anyway? Will your friends assume that you are sexually active just like your brother or sister? Will they think that you have the disease too?

Your anger and embarrassment are additional fallout of a sibling's sexual activity. The anger may be directed at your brother or sister or at your parents or even at God. Sam was deeply affected by what happened to Tami. He never forgave Al for what happened. As a result, anger consumed Sam for the rest of his life.

How Do You Handle Anger?

How do you release this type of anger if you are the innocent party, the one who didn't have sex? If you have had sex, how do you let go of anger at the one who pressured you to have sex? Or, hardest of all, how do you handle anger at yourself for giving in?

First, remember that anger itself is not a sin. It is an emotion. It is a symptom, like pain, telling you something is out of whack. The feeling is not wrong but it can lead to wrong actions.

Express your anger. I'm not suggesting you go around shouting and slamming doors so everyone knows you are mad. Tell someone . . . God, a trusted friend, and, if possible, the person who angered you. If you don't express your resentment, that person may not even be aware of what he or she has done.

Decide to forgive the person who made you angry, even if that person is yourself. Forgiveness is something you do, not something you feel. Feelings take time to heal, but you can speed the process by recognizing the anger when it returns and using it as a reminder to pray for that person. When I do this, I find that one of two things may happen: Either I stop getting angry or my prayer life improves. Either way I win!

But what if you are the one who was sexually active and your actions have hurt others? In the last chapter, we talked about breaking the news to your parents that you were going to have a baby. Now imagine announcing the event to your younger brother or sister.

How will you feel when your younger brother or sister follows in your footsteps? What if they become sexually active too? Maybe you didn't get a disease, but they do. Will you feel responsible?

If your brother or sister is already aware of your past sexual behavior, perhaps they are angry. Think about asking him or her to forgive you and then tell them about renewed virginity.

If you wait for sex until you are married, you will never have to face these issues. In fact, if you remain sexually pure, your younger brother or sister may choose to follow your example.

Sharon exults, "My sister was still a virgin when she married at age twenty-one. Not only that, the fellow my sister married had never had sex. He was twenty-seven! Now I've decided to wait too!"

"Wait a minute, here," you say. "Suppose I decide not to have sex and I finally meet the person of my dreams. Then I discover that he or she already had sex with someone else. If I wait, doesn't God owe it to me to give me someone who hasn't had sex?"

With so many young people being sexually active today, finding out your date is a renewed virgin is a real possibility. Yet I meet many young people who tell me they only want to marry a virgin. After all, they kept themselves pure. Don't they deserve a marriage partner who is also pure? That seems only fair.

If this were true, what hope would there be for the person who is a renewed virgin? Did God really make him or her new, or do renewed virgins still have only second-class status?

The answer to that question depends in part on you. From God's perspective, the renewed virgin is first class. He or she is a completely new creation. But from a human perspective, the answer depends on you. Will you be bitter and reject that person, or will you forgive him for what he did in the past?

Before my husband, Gene, and I met, he had been sexually intimate with other people. He was nervous as he revealed his past to me. He wondered how I would react. My response? I said, "Gene, God knew all about your past before He led us together. He knew all about you and all about me. If God in His wisdom picked you, out of all the men available in this world, for me to marry, who am I to question His choice? I trust His wisdom to give me the very best."

How could I reject the man whom God chose for me and say, "No, God, he must be a virgin"? Could I set my standards higher than God's?

I've talked to Christians who say that they could never marry someone who had been sexually active, someone who came from a broken home or someone who had been abused. They tell me, "I'm afraid I couldn't deal with all that emotional baggage."

Can a person truly become new again? Yes. Is divorce really contagious? No. Does abuse have to repeat itself in the next generation? No. Is God as powerful to change old patterns as people claim He is? The answer is a resounding YES! My husband is a perfect illustration of God's ability to take someone from the scratch-and-dent pile and turn him into someone brand new. For that matter, so am I. Sure, I was a virgin when I married, but I was not perfect or flawless. My sin wasn't sexual, but God had to make me into a fresh creation too, to make me fit for Gene.

Only after God made us both new did He put us together. He knew that together we would be able to serve others who have been scratched and dented by this world.

Tami's brother, Sam, was bitter. He wanted justice, but he wanted it in his own time and on his own terms. God is just, but what Sam never understood was that God's timing is often different than our own. He has infinite patience and the divine ability to change a person.

God transformed Gene and me; He could have changed Sam too. He could have taken away Sam's pain and anger, but Sam never let Him.

Will you?

1. What would you say to your brother/sister if he/she became sexually active?

2. Who looks up to you and follows your example? Hebrews 12:13 says, "Mark out a straight path for your feet. Then those who follow you, though they are weak and lame, will not stumble and fall but will become strong."

3. Go back to the questions at the end of chapter 3. Read Second Corinthians 5:16-17 again. What areas of your life (sexual or not) need to be changed by God?

4. What hurts in your past control you, like Sam, and keep you from serving God today?

Other Thoughts

On the next page, write a letter to your brother or sister explaining why you want them to wait for sex until marriage.

REAL LiFE

Tamara Mowery of *Sister, Sister*

Tia and Tamara Mowery have the special fortune to be sisters both in real life and on stage. They are also bonded by a commitment to wait for sex until marriage.

Tamara says, "We saw the True Love Waits convention—Through the Roof—on the Trinity Broadcasting Network. We're making that same kind of commitment—to save sex for marriage—because that's what Christ wants. And, personally, I just think that's the best way. . . .

"People think we're crazy, but I don't even have the desire to date right now. School is more important, and we just don't have time. We think guys are cute, but we don't want serious relationships right now. . . .

"Tia and I always mention Christ in the interviews that we do. Everywhere we go and every speech we make, the first thing that comes out is that we're Christians. We mention it on talk shows because we're not afraid to tell anyone that we're Christians and that we think sex should come after marriage, and that Christ is the No. 1 person in our lives. We are not ashamed."

Quoted portions are from "Tia and Tamara" by Susie Shellenberger, *Brio* magazine, July 1996, published by Focus on the Family. Copyright 1996 by Focus on the Family. All rights reserved. International copyright secured. Used by permission.

five

A Friend Speaks

"I had no idea that all this would happen. I mean, I didn't think anyone would get hurt. Everything just seemed to snowball.

"I was Al's best friend. When Al told me how he felt about Tami, I thought he was nuts, but I thought I'd help him out since he seemed so worked up about it. So, I told him to pretend he was sick and get her up to his room. We worked it out so he was alone with her. But I never imagined that this could ever happen!

"Maybe I figured he'd see her and come to his senses. Or maybe he'd eventually marry her. Only, Al didn't stop and he didn't marry her.

"I felt really sick when he pushed Tami out in the hall. There she was, crying. Her blouse was torn. I knew that I had to get her out of there as fast as possible. There wasn't time to think.

"Later Al refused to talk about it. He went on just like nothing had happened. I think I hurt more than he did. Like, if this is what he did to the girl he said he loved, what would he do to a friend? Tami trusted him, and look what happened. Why should I trust him?

"Well, pretty soon we didn't talk about much of anything anymore. I got to know Tami's brother, Sam, better, and Al and I drifted apart. It was sad 'cause we grew up together and had been best friends for as long as I could remember. It's crazy—you spend so much time with a person and then discover you never really knew him.

"How could so much happen because of one stupid act? No one ever told me anyone could get hurt, let alone be killed. I lost my best friend and now Sam is gone too."

Sex Can Separate Friends

Jon never expected that his off-the-cuff suggestion would result in so many problems. Perhaps he himself had already been sexually active and gotten away with it—nobody got pregnant, nobody got a disease. But when Al raped Tami, Jon sobered up. It hurt to see Tami cry. It hurt to lose his best friend. It hurt to see Sam not talk to Al for over two years.

Al's dad had a friend too, remember? After Al's dad went to bed with his friend's wife, that friend was killed just like Al. The sad part was that the friend hadn't done anything to deserve it. Sometimes innocent parties get hurt.

Sexual intimacy has a way of wounding friends on the periphery as well as those involved in the physical act of sex.

Doug lost two of his friends when they became sexually active. Doug, "Traci" and "Ben" were in the same youth group at church. When Traci and Ben began dating each other, they had just begun high school. By the time they were seniors, Traci and Ben were sleeping together. They reasoned that this was not casual sex. It had taken a long time to reach that level of intimacy.

After graduation, Ben, Traci and Doug all went to different colleges. Long-distance relationships were hard to keep up. Ben decided he wanted to date other girls at his campus. Having already been sexually active with Traci, Ben found his new relationships quickly became physical. After a few weeks, he was in bed with another girl.

Over Christmas break, Doug went home and saw Traci at church. "When I asked her how Ben was doing, Traci burst into tears. She told me how one weekend she traveled up to see Ben at his campus. They went to bed together one more time. Then she heard that Ben had been having sex with the other girl. Traci was crushed. Even though she and Ben were not officially dating anymore, it hurt her to know that Ben had moved so rapidly into another intimate relationship."

Doug wanted to console Traci but Ben expected Doug to take his side. "Suddenly I found myself torn between comforting Traci and being loyal to Ben. Each of them expected me to be on their side. Now, I've lost two friends. They're both mad at me."

"When I was in high school," says Jenna, "one of my girl-friends began to date a guy in her class. 'Susan' wanted to be with him all the time. Her parents didn't approve and started setting limits on the time Susan spent with this guy."

Susan argued that it wasn't fair. Why didn't they trust her? She began to see her boyfriend behind her parents' backs. She'd tell her mom, "I'm over at Jenna's house studying," but really she'd be out with her boyfriend. Their relationship evolved, and soon they were sexually active.

One night, Susan's mother called Jenna's house at 11:00 p.m. and asked to speak with Susan. Jenna was surprised. "I hadn't spoken to Susan for over a week. She was always busy with her boyfriend. So when her mom called me that night, I explained that Susan wasn't at my house, nor had she come over to study earlier."

When Susan discovered her secret was out, she became angry with Jenna. Susan had lied to her folks and expected

Jenna to cover for her. Jenna recalled, "I felt like she was using me and was not really my friend. We didn't see much of each other after that."

Susan didn't change her behavior. She kept seeing the same guy but now she told her parents she was with other friends. Gradually all her friends started to withdraw. No one wanted to be around her when she lied. At the time it didn't bother Susan. After all, she was still with the guy.

Then her boyfriend left. Susan was brokenhearted. She wasn't pregnant, but she was crushed. Jenna says, "And there were no friends left to help her pick up the pieces. She had driven us all away."

Scott, like Jenna, found that a friend's sexual behavior tore apart a good relationship. When he was a senior in high school, Scott and "Tim" went to Europe on a school trip. Tim was dating a girl at their school, and before he left on the trip, Tim told her he loved her and that she was his only girl.

"While we were in Germany, Tim started hanging around with one of the girls on the trip," Scott recalled. "One thing led to another, and pretty soon they were in bed together. When we got back to school, Tim boasted to all of us guys about what he'd done, but I noticed he never told his girlfriend."

As Scott evaluated the episode, he thought, "If this is what he does behind the back of the girl he says he loves, what would he do behind my back? Can I really trust him?" Shortly after that the guys were no longer friends, even though they had known each other a long time.

Jenna valued honesty and lost a friend because Susan's sexual activity led to lies. Scott thought trust was important and was disillusioned when Tim cheated on his girlfriend.

Julie's friend "Kara" became pregnant but hid the fact from everyone. For months Kara carried the lonely secret. Her parents never knew. Julie found out only after the baby was born. "Why didn't she tell me?" Julie asks. "I would have helped her.' After all, what are friends for?"

Julie was sad because her friend didn't share her problem. And, after being hurt by the guy she was dating, Kara no longer knew who her real friends were.

Doug, Jenna, Scott and Julie didn't have sex, but each lost a friend when that friend became sexually intimate with someone else.

Sex Complicates Communication

Sex has a way of complicating other aspects of friendship. For example, a sense of humor.

Jen, "Beth" and "Marie" planned to wait for sex until marriage. Then a rumor spread around school that Marie had been in bed with one of the football players. When the three girls got together, Jen and Beth joked about the rumor. Jen recalls, "We joked with Marie about it because we knew it couldn't be true. We were certain Marie would never have done something like that. We wanted Marie to laugh with us, but she couldn't . . . the rumor was true." After an embarrassed silence, there wasn't much for the girls to laugh about.

What about communication between friends? Does sex change that too? Imagine you have been sexually intimate with one person. You break up. Later you meet the person you want to marry. You fall madly in love. Then you discover that your future spouse is the roommate of the first person you slept with. Will you tell your future marriage partner that you were once in bed with his or her best friend? How will you feel as you look into the eyes of the one you love and tell him or her something like that?

Perhaps it would be easier not to talk about it. If you don't tell your future spouse about your past, what will happen when he or she hears about it from their former roommate instead? Will this change his or her ability to trust you? Will it create tension in his or her friendship with that former roommate?

In one rural high school in Pennsylvania, 200 seniors signed up to give blood as part of a blood drive. Over sixty of these student donors were rejected when their blood tests indicated they were HIV-positive. Students who already knew they were infected did not sign up for the blood drive, so these sixty students were ones who had no clue that they might be infected. After all, they had only had sex with friends they had known all their lives. But one of those "friends" had HIV and never bothered to tell them.

Does sex affect communication? You bet.

Pam, who told me about the school just mentioned, says, "My boyfriend was one of the sixty who found out they had HIV. He had the guts to tell me, even though he knew I was not at risk. You see, long before we dated, I made a choice not to have sex." Four years later, Pam's boyfriend died. The following May, Pam walked across the stage and received her college diploma. One little decision to wait for sex until marriage made a difference between life and death, though she did not know it at the time.

When your friends start having sex, it puts additional pressure on you. Hey, if they are doing it, maybe everyone is. How do you resist that pressure? If you are smart, you choose friends who also want to wait for sex until marriage and who won't lean on you to give in.

What if friends you care about become sexually active? Keep communication going by being honest with them. Let them know the risks—not just pregnancy or disease, but how it might affect your friendship. Don't preach, but tell them in a way that shows how much you think of them and value their friendship. If they know you really care, your friends may trust you enough to seek your help when they need it.

Jon helped set the scene for Al to rape Tami. He felt terrible after he saw how it hurt Tami and changed his friendship with Al. I wonder what would have happened if Al had had a real friend.

Chew On It:

1. Who are your best friends? What qualities stand out in your relationship with them?

2. How would you feel if your best friend became sexually active? Would you talk with him or her about it? What would you say?

3. Proverbs 27:6 says, "Wounds from a friend are better than many kisses from an enemy." How do you think this applies to talking with your friends about their sexual behavior?

4. Which of your friends might help you stand strong against pressures to give in to hormones?

Other Thoughts

Has a friend of yours become sexually active? Tell the story here and describe how it has affected your friendship. (Again, I suggest being careful with names in case you loan out this book.)

REAL LiFE

A.C. Green, NBA basketball player with the Miami Heat

A.C. Green currently holds the NBA's "Iron Man" title, having played in 1,192 consecutive games. Accomplishing this feat has taken a lot of strength and perseverance on his part. Similarly, his stand on waiting for sex until marriage has required a lot of grit.

"In high school I had relationships that never resulted in sex. But that's not what I told people. Most of the guys I hung around with pressured me to have sex to be included with the homeboys. Like a lot of kids I talked a lot even though nothing happened. . . . I had the guys fooled that I was 'doing it,' and they had me fooled that they were too.

"When my friends were telling me how much fun I was missing out on, the grace of God kept me. It wasn't that I didn't want to have sex or didn't think about it, but my self-respect never broke down."

In 1991 his teammate Earvin "Magic" Johnson tested positive for HIV. A.C. struggled when he heard what had happened to his friend. "My stomach felt hollow, like the center of my body had just been cut out. I started crying.

"I couldn't pray enough. It was an endless day, an endless prayer, an endless searching, why God would allow such a thing. For five years I'd spent almost every day with [Earvin]. For five years I had prayed every day for God to work in his life. Now this. . . . The only thing I could do in this situation was to love my friend, to blanket him with love.

"The real tragedy in Earvin's announcement is that something like this happens, yet people don't learn the lesson. A great man is down. But people continue in the same behavior. And that hurts me as much as anything.

"Most of my teammates went in for testing when they heard. Not me. It was one of the most traumatic experiences of my life, but I knew I was disease-free. The way I've chosen is the best way. I've been criticized and ridiculed, but I am not afraid to stand alone on this issue."

Quoted portions are from A.C. Green, *Victory* (Lake Mary, FL: Creation House, 1994), pp 129-131, 211-213. Used by permission.

six

God Speaks

"I was there when Al raped Tami. Al thought that nobody saw what had happened, but I was there.[1]

"You know, sex was my idea in the first place. Long ago, I said it is not good for man to be alone. I made a woman to be his companion.[2] When the first man and woman had sex, I approved.[3] They lay naked next to each other without shame.[4] Nothing was hidden. When the woman became pregnant, it was with my help.[5]

"Things changed. Men weren't content with one wife. They took women that didn't belong to them.[6] They desired women who were married to other men.[7] One man wanted to have sex with his mother; another went to bed with his sister.[8]

"When Al forced Tami into his bed, I wasn't shocked. It wasn't the first time this happened.[9] But some people thought because it wasn't the first time, I didn't care. I do. I hurt every time I see one of my children hurting another of my children. My eyes are like a fountain that constantly flows with tears. Sometimes I wish I could go away and forget the people I made. I'd live in a shack in some deserted place and not have to deal with their sin."[10]

God Thought Up Sex

When two people have sex outside the bond of marriage, it is never a private event. It hurts each person's relationship with a future spouse. As we have seen in the previous chapters, it affects their relationship with parents, brothers, sisters and friends as well. But sometimes we forget how it hurts God too. Sin stabs Him in the gut. It is like a nail driven through a tender wrist joint.

A lot of people are afraid of God. They see Him as the wrathful God of judgment. They think He sits up in heaven watching, ready to zap you if you step out of line. They think He is against sex.

Would it surprise you to discover that God is the author of sex? He's the one who thought up the idea of sex so that we could enjoy intimacy in marriage.

When God created the world He made the sun and the moon, and He said, "This is good." Then He made the land and the sea. Again He said, "This is good." He shaped the birds, the fish, the hippopotami and the fleas. After each creation was completed, He looked at it and said, "This is good."

Finally He made man and woman. What do you think He said next? "Whoops! This was a real mistake. Back to the drawing board."

No, when God made man and woman He was excited. He exclaimed, "This is *very* good!" (Genesis 1:31, author paraphrase). In other words, when God made us male and female, He was saying, "This is my best idea yet!"

God could have made us like earthworms. If you remember your high school general science course, you'll recall that every earthworm has both male and female sexual organs. God, as Creator, made earthworms unisex, and He had the skill to do the same with us. But He didn't. He made each of us either male or female. Why? Because He thinks sex is great. To use His words, it is "very good."

You say, "Big deal. He chose to make dogs male and female too." You're right, but God made us different from dogs and cats. He made us in His image. Just as He yearns for intimacy in a relationship with His children, He made us crave intimacy. Sexual desires are a physical expression of our need for intimacy.

God knows that intimacy between two people involves a lot more than two bodies fitting together. When you see two dogs sniffing each other and then five minutes later mating, would you call that a relationship? Not likely.

Sex Is God's Gift

When God made us, He wanted so much more for us. He tied our physical and emotional responses together. He knew the pain that results from jealousy, anger and broken trust. For sex to be as good as God planned it to be, He said it must be within the context of marriage. That rule was not to make life difficult for us; it was to protect us and to allow us to enjoy sexual intimacy at its best.

One day, a young man asked me, "If God wanted us to wait for marriage to have sex, why did He give us all these hormones before marriage?" (Actually, his question was a lot more frank than that!)

The question is a fair one. Why does God give us strong sexual desires before marriage? As Creator, He could easily have designed the wedding night as the trigger that released our sexual hormones. But He didn't plan it that way.

Do we picture God handing out sexual passions to young people and then gleefully telling them not to satisfy those desires until marriage? Is He up in heaven laughing and saying, "It is so much fun to watch them struggle!"? Is God cruel, like a parent who gives his child a wonderful toy and then tells the child that he can't play with it? A lot of young people think God is like that when it comes to sex.

If God is not some kind of divine spoilsport, why in the world did He give us sexual passions and then ask us to wait? God knew that practice at refusing sexual temptation before marriage was essential if we were to develop skills for dealing with sexual temptation after marriage. He also knew that if you have sex outside marriage, you will get hurt. You will hurt not because God is mean, but because God is just. He built into this world natural consequences for wrong actions. Every year God grieves over millions of unmarried women who fall apart when their pregnancy tests give a positive result. He anguishes over young men who discover firsthand that herpes is a lifelong disease—they won't be able to trade in their bodies at 100,000 miles for a new model. He listens to the angry fights of couples whose marriages are torn apart by betrayal. These wounds are the ordinary results of personal choices to disregard God's plan to keep sex within marriage.

God Is Just

One time a man told me, "I believe God is loving, He is merciful, He is forgiving. No loving God would make a young girl carry a pregnancy to term and force her to care for a child, messing up the rest of her life, because she made one mistake."

"You are right that God is loving. He is merciful. He is forgiving," I agreed. "But where in your picture of God do you fit His justice? Where are His righteous standards? What about His holiness?"

You can't have only part of God. He is not like a smorgasbord where you pick and choose what He is like. A little kindness, yes. A lot of love, please. No, thank you, I'll pass on the judgment. We may want to put a big helping of God's justice on other people's plates, but not on our own. Most of us want a just God, a God who will deal with murderers and thieves. We want God to judge people like Al who hurt innocent people like Tami. But what many people don't realize is that any sexual relationship outside marriage, even when two people mutually agree to do it, is offensive to God. It is against His plan.

You see, marriage is a picture of Jesus' relationship to the Church. Jesus is the groom, the Church is the bride (Ephesians 5:23-33). Just as that relationship is pure and holy, God wants the marriage relationship between a man and woman to be pure and holy. God's command to wait for sex until marriage is an expression of His love. Far from being a wall to keep you from having fun, God's law is a barrier to protect you from being hurt. He warns you about what will happen if you step outside His plan, but He leaves the final choice up to you.

Many choose to ignore God's warning. Those who do get hurt.

Is there a way to get back on track? Yes. God may not take away physical consequences like the pain of genital warts. He might not keep a woman from getting pregnant to avoid embarrassment for her or her family. But God can take away the emotional and spiritual consequences. He does extend forgiveness to people like Al. He will give strength to live again to young women like Tami.

God Sees

Some people think God doesn't see and He doesn't care when we ignore His plan.

Each year at the college where my husband teaches, one of the sociology professors gives an assignment to his class: Go and break one social norm and observe how people react. It might be something like wearing pajamas to the cafeteria or talking too loudly in a conversation.

For her assignment, Brooke sought out a dormitory lounge. There a young man was kissing his girlfriend as they sat on the couch. Arms wove the two figures into a single embrace. Until they noticed Brooke. Brooke took a seat and began to stare at the couple.

Slowly their arms loosened. Brooke continued to gaze at them. The young man sat up a bit straighter. The girl tucked her blouse in. Brooke kept staring. They moved a little further apart on the couch. Brooke's eyes never wavered.

Silence weighed upon the room. Nervous looks passed between the couple. They whispered a comment or two and then fell silent again. Brooke inspected them with undivided attention.

Finally, the couple stood up and walked toward the exit. Brooke's eyes followed them across the room. Only when they reached the door did Brooke jump up and approach them. Barely able to control her laughter, she explained her class assignment to the offended couple. Their icy indignation melted as they realized how having an observer had affected their behavior.

God is your silent observer on every date. He may not be as obvious as Brooke was, but He is just as surely there. He is not rude. He doesn't intrude. But He is there. Many people try to hide from His sight. One person wrote, "Where can I get away from God's presence? If I get up early in the morning and I flee to the far side of the earth, even there God will be near me. If I try to hide in a dark room, if I turn out the light, even the darkness is not dark to God" (Psalm 139:7-12, author paraphrase).

Do you think that the One who made our eyes can't see? Is it possible that the One who invented ears cannot hear? (Psalm 94:8-9; Isaiah 59:1).

God Is Concerned

Others pretend that even if God sees, He doesn't care. They do something they know is wrong, and then they try to buy God off by throwing a couple of dollar bills in the offering plate on Sunday morning. To them God says, "You think this is OK? Try it on your girlfriend! Give her gifts like that after you've betrayed her and see how pleased she is!" (Malachi 1:8, author paraphrase).

How can you say that the Lord doesn't care? (Isaiah 40:27). Does God care when you break a leg on the ski slope, when you are physically in pain? How much more will He care when your heart is torn in two by a broken relationship?

If God really cared, you may ask, how could He let Al rape Tami? Where was God when Tami needed help? Perhaps He was taking a nap. Perhaps He was out on a coffee break, and when He came back, He said, "Whoops! Look what happened while I was getting a doughnut!"

No, God knew what happened. He was there. And He cared. Funny way of showing He cared, you say? You are right. Many books have attempted to answer the question of

why bad things happen to innocent people. I've listed a few
of these books at the end of the chapter. The answer is not an
obvious one—much of it comes down to simple faith. We
just have to have faith that God knows what He's doing.

For me, the answer keeps coming back to basic facts about
God's character. First, He doesn't make mistakes. Second,
He loves us enough to give us freedom to make bad choices.
Third, He is powerful enough to heal wounds inflicted by
those who make wrong choices.

God loved Al. He gave Al a choice to follow Him or his hormones, and would have forgiven Al if he had asked. God loved
Tami and offered her healing and strength to go on. He can do
the same for you, no matter what has happened in your life.

Here are some additional resources that discuss why God
allows bad things to happen in this world:

Dobson, James. *When God Doesn't Make Sense*. Carol
    Stream, IL: Tyndale House Publishers, 2001.
Jacobs, Joy. *When God Seems Far Away*. Camp Hill, PA:
    Christian Publications, Inc., 2000.
Lewis, C.S. *The Problem of Pain*. San Francisco: Harper San
    Francisco, 2001.
Yancey, Philip. *Where is God When it Hurts?*. Grand Rapids,
    MI: Zondervan Publishing House, 2001.
Yancey, Philip. *Disappointment with God*. Grand Rapids, MI:
    Zondervan Publishing House, 1997.

1. God is with you each time you go out on a date. How does knowing this affect the boundaries you set for physical intimacy?

2. Read the following sentences and describe God's feelings when we disobey His commands.

> You have betrayed me . . . You have been like a faithless wife who leaves her husband. (Jeremiah 3:20)

> What should I do with you? . . . For your love vanishes like the morning mist and disappears like dew in the sunlight. (Hosea 6:4)

> I fed my people until they were fully satisfied. But they thanked me by committing adultery and lining up at the city's brothels. . . . Should I not punish them for this? (Jeremiah 5:7, 9).

3. In your own words, summarize why God wants you to
   wait for sex until marriage.

4. If you are hurting now because of things that happened in
   the past, what hope do the following sentences give for
   your future?

> I will give you back your health and heal your
> wounds. (Jeremiah 30:17)

> The Lord has called you back from your grief—as
> though you were a young wife abandoned by her hus-
> band. . . . For a brief moment I abandoned you, but with
> great compassion I will take you back. In a moment of an-
> ger I turned my face away for a little while. But with ever-
> lasting love I will have compassion on you. (Isaiah 54:6-8)

Other Thoughts

Think of someone you know who has become sexually active. How has his or her relationship with God changed?

Endnotes

1. Psalm 139:2-3, 11-12.
2. Genesis 2:18.
3. Genesis 2:24.
4. Genesis 2:25.
5. Genesis 4:1.
6. Exodus 20:14.
7. Exodus 20:17.
8. Leviticus 18:7, 9, 11.
9. Ecclesiastes 1:10.
10. Jeremiah 9:1-2.

REAL LIFE

Twila Paris, Christian musician

Twila Paris knew her husband for nine years before they got married.

"I treasure the fact that my husband is the only man I've ever given any of myself to physically. This is the only man I've ever been with. And I'm the only woman he's ever been with. Do you understand the security in that? There's never any weird comparisons going on here. I have absolutely no reason to get jealous or feel threatened.

"I can be totally vulnerable and completely secure, and he can too. That's the way God intended marriage to be—to embrace us, not threaten us.

"If you disobey God's laws together before you're married, then who's to say your husband won't disobey those laws after you're married? You'll always know he doesn't put a high premium on morality. And five or ten years after you're married, you'll wonder, 'Is he having an affair?'

"Jack and I were alone in a car many times, but he never once tried anything. He had too much respect for God's laws and for me. Am I going to worry about this man ten years from now when I've had three kids and I'm not so attractive when someone else is? No. It's not going to matter how attractive someone else is, because it didn't matter ten years ago when I was more attractive.

"See how tight the bond of security is when you follow God's laws? When you cement a relationship with trust instead of physical intimacy, you're bonding forever."

The Story Ends:

Nothing but the Truth

 This book has told the story of two young people named Tami and Al. Names were changed, but the facts were all true. Now it is time to reveal the truth.

Let's begin with Al's dad. Al told you that his dad was internationally known as a military expert in the Middle East and that his dad was a big political figure over there. Al's dad's real name was King David, and he lived over 2,000 years ago. Godly King David of the Bible. Godly David who, with only a slingshot and a few stones, fought a giant named Goliath. Godly King David who wrote many of our favorite psalms. And godly King David who pressured Bathsheba, the wife of one of his closest friends (2 Samuel 11:3-4).

Al's real name was Amnon. Let's keep calling him "Al" just to keep things straight. Al was the son of David's second wife. Because David's first wife, Michal, never had children (6:23), Al was the crown prince. He was to inherit the throne after David died. And yes, Al raped Tami. Only I didn't mention that she was more than a family friend: She was his half sister (13:1-2).

Tami's brother, Sam, was actually called Absalom. Just as he said, he was never the same after Al raped Tami. He murdered Al (13:28). When that didn't soothe his anger and he still wanted to restore his sister's honor, he named his own daughter after her. Sam surrounded himself with people who had been hurt by rape. When he revolted against King David, Sam chose a cousin to lead his military campaign. This man, Amasa, was born because a man raped Sam's aunt. Sam's chief advisor was the grandfather of Bathsheba, the woman Al's dad forced into bed (17:25). And, most unbelievable of all, Sam ended up abusing women himself. He raped several women who had had sex with his father, but Sam didn't do it in private like his dad. He assaulted them out in public on the rooftop of the palace in Jerusalem! (16:22).

Jon was Jonadab. He wasn't just Al's friend. He also happened to be Al's cousin (13:3). You see, all these people were a close-knit family. Jon was the one who came up with the idea of Al pretending he was sick and getting Tami to come to his room (13:5). When Sam murdered Al, Jon was also the one who broke the news to David (13:32).

And Tami? Her real name was Tamar. David had nineteen sons but only one daughter (1 Chronicles 3:9). Daddy's only little girl. After Al hurt her, Tami never married. She lived with Sam for several years, but, after he murdered Al, Sam had to leave the country. Tami must have missed her brother terribly. After all, he had been her main support after the nightmare of her rape by Al. How do you think she felt when she learned that Sam raped other women? Do you think she wept when he died after trying to steal the throne from David?

Did Tami ever get justice from God after Al raped her? Yes. God recorded the truth in a book that would be read all over the world in hundreds of languages for more than 2,000 years.

The whole ugly history is right there in your Bible. You will find the story in Second Samuel 13.

Why Did God Tell This Story?

The only name in our story that wasn't changed was that of God. Why did God put such a horrible account in the Bible? The Bible is full of nice stories about godly King David. Why did God drag all this in from the gutter? After all, Al and Tami weren't even major characters in the book. God is in the business of truth. Nothing we do is hidden from His sight. Sooner or later, God always exposes the truth.

I believe there are two key reasons why these chapters are in the Bible.

1. Sexual desires are nothing new.

The story of Al raping Tami tells us that problems with sex have been around for thousands of years. All through history young people have had difficulty controlling their sexual passions. If you struggle with those hormones dashing around in your body, *you are normal*!

Each young person down through history has faced the same difficulty. Sexual passion wasn't just discovered ten years ago. It has been around a long time. The strong feelings you have today are not wrong or dirty. They are normal, God-given passions. It is just your turn to fight the battle for self-control.

2. Everybody struggles, not just you.

The second reason God put this story in the Bible is to show that not just ungodly people struggle with sexual hormones. God distributes sexual hormones to Christians and non-Christians alike. Imagine God sitting up in heaven. He looks down and says, "You see Joe there? He's a fine young man. He goes to church every Sunday. He sings in the choir and even helps out in the church nursery now and then. I don't want him to struggle with temptation. I'll just give him a light dose of sexual hormones.

"But Sandi? You see her over there? Her home is a mess. Her mom's on drugs. Her dad's in jail. Sandi swears all the time. I'll just dump my surplus load of hormones in her direction. There's no hope for her anyway."

No! God's not like that. He gives hormones to everyone. He gives them to kids living in the streets of a Chicago slum. He gives them to the clean-cut farm boy from Idaho. God distributes hormones freely to people with curly hair and with straight hair, to tall people and short people. He passes out passions in godly homes and ungodly homes. We all get a share. A baptismal certificate is not an inoculation against temptation. Perfect attendance at your youth group will not make you invincible to hormonal attraction.

King David's home was no different. Just because David was a godly man and a king didn't change his DNA. The hormones that caused David to rape Bathsheba were passed on to his sons Al and Sam. And to another son called Solomon. Solomon had so much testosterone that he ended up with 700 wives! (1 Kings 11:3).

God doesn't condemn you for having hormones. After all, He gave them to you! And He put this story of Tami and Al in the Bible so you'd know that what you are facing is normal and so you'd see how much trouble uncontrolled sex can cause.

God's not against sex. In chapter 6 we discussed the fact that God created sex. He wants us to enjoy sex within marriage. Your hormones are a gift from Him to you. He gave you these hormones so you could enjoy awesome intimacy with your husband or wife.

The story of Tami and Al helps us understand why God tells us to wait for sex until marriage. Not because God is mean and enjoys watching us struggle with temptation, but because God is good. He treasures you and doesn't want you to be hurt. God is *for* you, not against you!

This is the kind of God you could fall in love with. In fact, all of Scripture is an unveiling of who God is. God wants us to know Him and love Him.

No matter how high you set your standards for your future mate, no one will ever be perfectly honest, flawlessly faithful, perfectly trustworthy, unfailingly patient . . . except God. No man or woman can ever love you in the future as much as God does right now.

The Choice Is Yours

Will you follow God or your hormones?

It is not a decision I can make for you. I already made a decision to put God first in my life long ago. I chose to follow God's plan. I waited for sex until I got married. I'm glad I did.

Now you are in the driver's seat. Your parents can't make this decision for you. They aren't with you all the time to check up on you. Your teacher or youth group leader can't give you an assignment: "Go home and be abstinent."

Only you can decide how you will deal with your hormones.

Waiting—the Smart Choice

Many young people have contributed to this book their stories and ideas of how they stayed in control. Maybe their stories will help you succeed where David, Al and Sam failed. I asked the young people who helped me why they chose to wait for sex until they married. Here are some of their answers:

"I'm a Christian," Gina says. "I believe God is wise. When He says He wants me to wait, I figure He knows best."

Doug told me, "As I see it, giving my virginity to my wife is one way I can show her I love her. I want to be able to look at my wife and tell her, 'I loved you even before I knew you. I saved myself for you.'"

Chad adds, "The way I look at it is, when I meet the woman of my dreams—the woman I want to marry—I'll want to give her something special to show her I love her. I could give her flowers. But Doug here, he could give her flowers too. I could give her candy . . . but Doug could give her candy also. I could marry her and give her a wedding ring. That would be special, right? But Doug could do the same. The way I figure it, the only thing I can give my wife that no other man can give her is my virginity."

Tara reasons, "I'm in college now. I have lots of goals for my-self. With all the pressure of exams, papers and classes, I don't need the extra stress that comes from being sexually active."

Kipp recently graduated. He's still waiting. "Frankly, I don't want to share my wife with other men. If I want her to wait, I figure she deserves the same respect from me."

One thing is clear. God loves you and gives you free will. You can choose His way or your own. The story of Tami and Al makes it clear that if you choose to have sex outside marriage, many people will be hurt. Not just your parents or your girl-friend or boyfriend or your brother or sister or your pals, but you. The choice is yours. What will you do?

Chew On It:

1. Have you been hurt by someone close to you who be-came sexually active? How would forgiving him or her help you heal?

2. Read the paraphrase of First Thessalonians 4:3-5 on the
   following page aloud. Think about what the verse is saying and record your thoughts in the space provided.

   > God wants *me* to be holy, so *I* should keep clear of all
   > sexual sin. Then *I* will control *my* body and live in holi-
   > ness and honor.

3. What is your personal decision about sexual purity before marriage? Express your decision in writing, sign it,
   make a copy and ask someone you trust to keep it in a
   safe place.

4. What practical steps can you take to help you remain sexually pure?

Other Thoughts

Try writing a letter about yourself to your future spouse.
Would you prefer to tell the person you love about how you
waited for him or her or about how you were hurt in past relationships?